Heart of Earth

*Tale
and the Precious
Moments*

For my great teachers
for those lucky ones
still feeling something fair
in their heart
And, for those blessed
still, believing to a natural wisdom
beyond our understanding
A small bow, that lies, under thy feet

ARTHUR WOODLANDS

HEART OF EARTH

TALE
AND THE PRECIOUS
MOMENTS

© 2017 Arthur Woodlands
Publisher: BoD – Books on Demand, Helsinki, Finland
Producer: BoD – Books on Demand, Norderstedt Germany
ISBN: 978-951-568-118-8

Poems, How the Story Goes?

Follow the Tale

— Poems for youth
and, for elders
anyone
A head on shoulders —

Once in a While
Stay Low
And Live Slow
Take All the Time
Stay Alive

Heart

Earth

Art

Tale – Intro

So, soon an adventure will begin. But, first few words for your delight, so you can prepare for the world you are entering.

As a reader, you have few choices here. The novel, and the tale, is a collection of poems. You can either follow the tale from the first page to the last, or you can select a poem, or two, suiting for your mood. Poetry is a world of rhymes, and speaking the sound out. It is the world of feelings, compelling ideas and metaphors, just not to forget the drama and philosophy. Hence, expect always only one thing: behind one story is another, over another, which just might hide another – making each poem also a riddle. This makes things more interesting – check the levels you can catch, and then dive deeper! It is worthwhile, and sometimes it might make you wish for a cigarette – even you wouldn't smoke. Take a short warm up, to the language used, by reading the poems: *Soul of the Story* & *Forging the Words*.

And then, a second thing before starting the timeless trip, it is just a great pleasure to introduce to you the hero of the story in the poem: *Sign for a Traveler*.

Soul of the Story

A letter and a space
a word and a rhyme
flooding over the line

A poem on the other
a story hiding a tale
each sinking
with the world spinning
an old book inking

Almost like a crime
for a moment
stealing the time
... of thy life

Forging the Words

A blacksmith forging
and, a crafting stonemason
a timberjack out, sawing in the woods
and a soldier, marching
till a spring, turns to June

There is a peace, between wars
and remember
a word, in a world
Please, read
the way
which, dead is written
A word is alive
red, a flow of blood
and white, all the colors
A starry, black night, after the other

Welcome, a world, of a living word!

Sign for a traveler

Thereafter
    within these covers
        since, the first page opens
I am you, and you are I
    it is a weird thing
        but, that is how we, here, survive ...

And please
    be always aware
        carefully take care
The devious devil
    probably sister of pure evil
        hiding, behind each line
            diving, into every rhyme
Good luck, and farewell!

Here, an odd journey begins ...

How It Started

Tale I – The Beginning

Every story has a beginning, now you are at one. A small suggestion here: give a look to the surroundings, touch the surface of earth, and take a deep breath. And please, do it all again, if you ever come back, here into the beginning. Hold a hand on your heart, for a while, till you feel its beat and power outside. Then seat back, touch your head and hair, hold your breath, here you go ... to a day, when it all began.

Garden

Once upon a time
   it all began
      in a garden
Man having an apple
   and, seeing
      a wormhole, staring

Straight trough
   he saw
      and, far beyond
All turning around
   an ancient wound
      on earth's ground

And, he was vanished
   then, found again
      out of the forgotten garden

On a shore, of a small lake

Not the same man
anymore
more of a fisherman, now
Having his first catch
a pike, perhaps
young fish
behind the strangest eyes

And, a hold to a knife
removing the hook
spike out of the mouth
But, there was something
that said, no
wait, hold on

Maybe, it was the innocence
or, something sacred
the virgin nature
We are not able to explain
rather
a choice, is to believe
The pike
being a messenger
old wisdom, in its eyes
Belonging, among the kinds

So, the tale tells
that, for saving her life
pike turned, eyes around
and gave a ring
for the fisherman
A golden, and silvering one
not on a finger
but only, for his sight
And speechless, was the man
let the pike, swim away

trough a blue mirror
into a different world

On a branch above
on a pine tree, not a dove
but a crow, was watching
trough golden rings
the sharpest, sun-like eyes
And as the pike disappeared
the black bird, dived
into air, above the lake
Swaying, up and down
cawing, aloud
what had been done
Perhaps blessing, the saved life

But, no one was hearing
and, no else saw
or, so the man first thought
All leaves of the forest
soon shaking, and waving
in a sudden blow
of a fierce wind
over, the serene waters
breaking, calm of air

Perhaps, someone heard
or saw
a kind thing, chosen
Blessed, he felt
against the wind
even, the catch had gone
And, fish into the waters, swum

Since then
every time, the fisherman
closed his eyes
a ring, turned around

A glimpse, into the garden
a wormhole leading
into the very beginning

You, Romeo

So, the man lived
now, in a small village
or, was it a town?
Anyway, a fisherman's paradise

And, did he tell
anyone
what he had found
from the waters, below
No, not even a word
about the strange pike
and, the odd treasure, given
A fool, someone would thought

Anyway, years passed by
and, in a normal way
also our man
finally, found
A loved one
someone nice
charming his lonely heart

So, this is the beginning
that man
now, being you
And, you telling
a strangest kind of a story
about a life on earth

Hey, here
*   in the beginning, just Romeo you are ...*

8

Heart, that Bleeds

*Blood is red
But, its wakes are white*

Tale II – Romeo

– So Romeo, sing while you can –

I am Alive

I am alive, so alive
    while, sailing the seas
    of thy eyes

Feel, the world
    whirling out
        out of the lips
        ... of thine

And, I always know
    I will never die
        ... I will never die
    Feel so alive

Road to Rome

This love is real
   the greatest liar
      ever, lived on earth
         whispered, into the air
There is a secret hole
   deep, in the heart
      the enchanted one, of thine
         a gateway, for your soul
         leading you to ...
The avenue of hope

The love is real
   share, all your trust
      take a leap, on me babe
It's faith
   here is my hand
      I'll be the guide ...

The avenue of hope
   Saints, on the streets
      Angels, on their feet
All pointing the way
   the sacred path
      for a believer, to take

Guiding you, to my home
   it is an ancient road
      dear, Amor
      a route
         into my heart's Rome

Diamonds

She is wearing, my diamonds
  would recognize em'
    anywhere
Ain't she a beauty?

In fact, there is nothing
  in this world, matching
    for the beauty
      of em' together
And the most, I hate the feeling
  going all mad, over em'
    stones, and jewels, of the jealous
If someone ... even dares
    God! not given em', just for spares

Ain't they heartbreaking
  eye shine -stealing
    the greatest treasure, on our earth
But, I'll be guarding
  forever, watching
    that is the thing, I was made for
Smelling the thieves
    and, all thoughts of steal
      even someone's will to kill
Ah, the stones burning, eyes of wary

My dear darling
  and, the precious one
    I want em' back, again
      it is not safe, not here
We should leave
  quite soon
    no, let's do it now
I feel, and sense
    they are coming

for those diamonds, of thine

Thief in Paradise

They stole it
they took it
under my eyes
I am sure
they have taken it

Thieves, and thieves
thieves, under my nose
nothing, but thieves
They have stolen
my darling
and, the precious ... diamonds

Tale III – The Way Down

So, the diamonds gone, and so is the loved one. A bit fast, but the time flies when you fall into the mysteries of love. Anyway, real deal, but that is – of course – not yet everything. On the moments like this, the greatness of humankind really shows the best. Now, let us see who were your friends, and who just kings, of jokers and fakes? Don't worry. It will always go like this. If there is even a smallest possibility, you are taken down. And now, some people – very close to you – have seen their fair chance to climb up a shiny stairway of the social hierarchy, by just pushing you down. Great is the will of climbing, and standing on your shoulders.

In general, nothing is better than a good and noble idea uniting people. It can create great goods. Sometimes, a novel idea spreads in speeds of bad news about awful catastrophe –

takes air under its huge wings, builds a religion-kind faith, and
soon all 'the fools on the sacred planet earth' will blindly follow
its views. Now, the noble thing uniting, just happens to be, taking
you down

Hence, the herald says
by insiders, by your friends
in the shadows of secrets
Conspiracy, will be your fate

from your hard-worked, and proved-to-be a fake, stand ...

Assassination

I have fallen
into the deepest thoughts
a friendship with frauds
A state of despair
only six, seven or five, miles
from a depression
Eternal desolation, slowly arriving

A meeting, to come
walking there, along the long line
with two friends, of mine
Wounded I am
a mental sort of scar
small, but severely bleeding
We are walking
the fragile line
of blind's despair
I between them
weight of the world
on my shoulders
double, the gravity

                dragging me down
        Too much, for one man to bear

Finally there
    meet em' all
        gathered to a hall
            seeing their smiles
                all fair, and shine
Oh, Jesus
        am I, blind?
            one having, even red teeth
                Judas, sharing his mark
    It is a holy miracle
            the wine
                turning to a red of blood
        Fellowers, of the dark hood

Shaking their hands
    the one, that is still free
        and the ones, that still dare
One can not have a doubt
        anyway
            my mind flown, already elsewhere
    Under a mist, I travel

Till I feel it
    it's a call to reality
        a surprise, even it was in the air
A warm stab
        into my back
            and another
                and another, after another ...
    Even you, my dear, Brutus the fair

And, I fall
    knives sticking, out of back
        what great gifts
            from dear friends

Of course, everyone wants to share
each, own precious dagger
being better, than anyone's else
the one thing uniting em'
It is a holy sacrifice, and a miracle

God, seems to make em' proud
strong, and above
what a great feeling, it must be
All the power, shared together

Besides, he deserved it
all too well
a bastard gone too proud
and, aloud
No one should, ever
step, on the might
of the brotherhood's pride
This is how we keep our faith pure
and lines straight

And I fall
onto the white of a marble floor
bleeding the red
more, than ever before
Can't still believe, why?
what did I do?
who did I fool?
No, it can not be true
even, it does not matter
no more

Now, I remember
god is fair, and merciful
but, the faith is blind
And so, might the humankind

Hear em' laughing

goodbye to remember
  still, only the steel is speaking
And, I bleed away
  see already my home
    all the red, on the white, marble floor

Tale IV – Last Smoke

So, you are done — anything to say, final words to share? Thank your friends, and loved ones. Might they hear? Take a smoke? The last one — even, you would not normally do such a spiritual thing — till you are finally gone ...

Bleeding Away

Hey, old and grey
  friend, and a wizard
    the great might, of the night
Let me, please
  taste, thy pipe
    for the final times

You see
  wounded, I am
    and my heart, bleeds out
See, all the scars
  and, the death
    waiting above
My end, was the Mars
  heart lost, into earthly wars

The cold comes
  sticks, into my bones
    freezes the mind

my shoulders go numb
and, down
I am bleeding, away
down to earth
so thirsty
always desiring
The red once stolen

I am done
enough, blood is gone
I leave now
with this last smoke
those small, white clouds
Farewell!

Can you still hear?
thank you, for the pipe
got my peace
anyway, you see
I am not here, no more
rather anywhere
gone, gone to my home
A route into the old, heart's Rome
It is fine, all fine
I am, with my kind

Here, no one blames
neither betrays
nor, tries to steal anything
Even know my name
greet, and smile
all, just a shine
I am with my kind

Death

Death arrived
not suddenly
nor, even squeezing
the breath away

It came
like a morning mist
over serene waters
Lingered
with the trees
and waited
Even shook their leaves
and rooted down
hiding underground
Waiting, and waiting

Thus, there is ...
only one thing
Sire, forever desires

Kind, of a Survival

Tale V – Lover's gone

So, the Romeo dead now, fell into love, and was betrayed, by the closest ones. But, the story – and life – must go on …

*Lover's gone
    Amor, wearing black
Greed, and lust of power
    far stronger
    Heil the Devil!*

*People teaming-up, for the good cause
    hating, the lucky ones
    endless form of envy
Or hey, pick the weak, and lone one
    all to beat, and rob
        together, we can make it
        so fair, and easy
And, when the great chance comes
    please, just prepare
        collection of knives, on the back*

Giant Rising

⸎ Spirit running free
nowhere to hold
flying and rising
soul is growing
Or twisting, and diminishing
into a deep, and dark
Good and evil, again, in a meeting ⸎

Lost Body

A body was found
by our faithful hound
in the middle of woods
wild, and pure, are the forestlands
Blood allover the shirt
holding the chest
face down, on dirt
Dead as man can be

It was there
on top that pretty little hill
A great view
but, who would ever kill?

Here, it was just here
where has it gone?
how's taken, him?
No signs of wolves
no howling, on these hoods
and, dead ain't walking

Even, in the old, wild woods?

Diamond Dagger

Digging, a dagger
*   deep, out of a bone*
*   of my thigh*

Graving, a memorial
*   on a gravestone*
*   over, the kingdom of mine*
*   diamonds on dagger, so fine*
Might blind, the sight of thine

And finally
*   when, the dead prey*
*   Sir, I am   ... on my way*

Giants

Hell with the people
*   and, their small wars*
I will rise, and escape
*   leave my sins*
*   the world, is yours*

Adios, small and kind
*   mean, and evil*
*   rising my hand, for the kind of thy*

A blessing from a heart
*   in pieces of a thousand, and one*

day will come
And thou, sand and sea, wilt see

Rising, and walking
leaves, on the ground
with a fierce wind, following
I need to grow
speak to the black of crow
till the giants show
start talking, so slow

It is a greater place
trees will speak
and, stones follow
a light wind, will blow
Believe, it is a leaf reader's world

With the wind, a word is spreading
on the air, now
'A new member, in the town
loyal, to the blue crown
... and, it will soon rain'
Giants smiling
'tears for thy poor soul
now light, and fair
... chose the right side'

I feel, no more pain
time flies
smaller me, dies
Now, only
a fair
... of god cries
Giants laughing

Ancients

Man, watching
   the wall of stones
      faces of ancients
         carving slowly out
Deep, from the woods
     one among, thousand trees
        million branches, and all the sprigs
    Guarding, a magnetic field
       a drop, at pressure of air, above
         and, sudden blow of wind
Carefully listen, the ancients speak

A Tree

A tree, I am
   next to you, I stand
      dear mirror, all shine of thine
         and still kind, of an opposite of mine
  Yet, for thee, just a tree

And here, I stand
   among my kind, within my nation
      under a green flag
         watching thee, running around, me
  Above
     seeing a nature of thine
        weighting, the kind of thy heart
  And, below
     judging, how you are tall
        your highness, what you are worth?
  There is a peace, in my world

Hear, a primeval call
    a magic, and a mystery
      mistress, lingering in a forest
The wild, walking the woodlands
    a wind, blowing through, the skin
      and all the heat, out bleeding
Now, shoulders down
    a shelter, and open heart, I am
      a green smile of the sun
        and a broken branch, foreseeing

And here I grow, and grace
    the sand and soil, under feet of thine
    and the air, you breathe
For thee, still, just a tree

Walk and be, feel thee, ye are aye free

Mister Woods

Mister Woods
    how's your moods
      things, under thy hoods?
Sharing some philosophy
    with the stones, again
      you never
        seem, to get enough
Wise, must you all be

I bet, a wet head, they told
    climb up, the stairs of airs
    and pray, for a day
Oh, had that same face
    many of thy age
      one of the thousands

you might say
And don't I love, too
the feeling
warmth, changing to cold
The young, slowly going, old

And, I hear
stand out, no fear
here, the peace, is always near
Please, look up, wards
take a breath
and, all the time
figure it out, my friend
E'er, you are, in expanding space

Turn thy heart out, you say
and promise, a day
the birds will come
Even the moon, towards
rising, till the sky falls
right, on your arms
All is good, under thy hood

Tale VI – Forest Elf

So, bigger man, now. That should be good, even ladies would prefer? And, in the wild woodlands, strangest things occur everyday. On a hill of a green valley, on a huge erratic boulder – stone sized of a house – an elf is sitting. Wood elf, of the primeval forest, following your slow hike trough the world of green. Old the elf must be, still appearing to be young, and cross-legged Indian style is a pose of the philosopher of the old woods. Smoking a peacemaker, something magical from the forestlands with a pretty nice scent, the white of clouds gliding down. And as you shadow-pace pass – now high and tall, raising a natural green hat he asks, to the open air and wind he speaks:

Mountain of Youth

Looking for a fountain
a spring, in a forest
a source of eternal youth?
Why won't you rise?
walk, and wander
the mountain, of truth?

If you are, lucky enough
may all those precious years
piled high, on the shoulders
Turn, back to days
seconds, and minutes
in the liveliest hours

A trail to remember
a grail, on the path
and, a young man, climbing
the final meters on
It is the top of the world

Thereafter
only dreams, of the youth
sliding down, the mountain
Years taken
all heavy, just forsaken
the peak, growing
Aye, loving em'

And, even ages later
only a thought
makes you young, again
The grail, never empties, in vain

Two Mountains

Between mountains, I lie
 two peaks
  and, all the heights
Watching, the higher altitudes
  uprising, elevations
   forcing to wonder
What are our rights?

The other
  so warm, and kind
   walls, closer to sun
And, the other
  more cool, and tempting
   shadows, making it steeper
Perfect, together they are

And, here
  under an oak, I lie
   don't know, where to go
Stuck between, halves the world
   frees the soul
    spirit rushing on the hillsides
Just like, the trees speak

The days roll over
  and the mounts, stand by
   master, the weather around
Change the winds
   gather the clouds
    keep the green, alive

And here
  with the magnificent tree, I lie
   shadows of the high valley, hide
    and, I dream

Finally, settling down

Lover Moon, what do you say?

* * * * * * * * * * * *

O', just a hollow, I am
roots, in the air
can't see, feel
I am with thee

Morning, on Mountains

Night, on a mountain
temps, below zero
icy frost, all over
And, a morning mist
lightness, of white shapes
ghosts, lost years and memories, rising
From the grounds, earth's small wounds
playing in the air
making the dance, visible for a while

A smoke
moist of the breath
both you
and, the mountain of two peaks
Under the fresh
of nature's high flesh
oh, my cold bones, it is a bless

And, a brook
melting of snow
a light purl teasing, and giggling around

Drops, running down
and finally, you own an idea
doing the same

Sayanora, a silent wish
back to the humankind
like turning the eye ring, of a fish
The one
you once saved a life, in the beginning

Blue Shield

Hey, Captain!
where is the shield?
The one
keeping your head, above

Watch out!
there is evil, in the air
eyes up, now

Take it, and wear it, please
keeps you safe
and, your soul pure

The blue
and, the star
onto thy left arm
Open sky, and the fair heart

Game of Diamonds

Tale VII – Comeback

As enlightened, not the same man anymore, a greater one, one could say. Now, coming down, back to the kind of our own, from his trails and travels, to the human's world, and to the people, living in the fisherman's village. Please, don't feel that you asperse the community too much, anyone coming from longer travels feels a bit the same - adaptation will take time. Anyways,

> Now, the Giant
>   kneeling down
>   to the heights, of our own
>   Man, growing his soul

And he, the man being you, is eventually drawn; back to our game, and to the most precious one ...

> Love, in its various disguises
>   forever desiring, what is hers

And he walks into a beautiful park; a green garden blooming on all the colors of spring that just freshly rose, underneath.

Caesars

Just a gaze
    cuts an arm
      and, the time escapes

A statue, at the park
    thumb up
      and, deep into the grounds
  You are dead, and so alive

Watch, what you do
    say, and are
      the judge, is here
  Weights, thy heart

Here, I kneel
    to the heights
      of youth
  Face the sun, and south

There is Caesar, in the park
    scissors, open
      stones, shall speak
        if any papers exist
          just full of beautiful bloom of lies
  Fading into the wind

Tale VIII – Fooled, again?

Time goes by, and finally, the giant in a smaller suit, finds an interesting one, someone charming his heart again. And, a game of love begins; where it always starts ...

>Hear, and listen, you fool!
>the lost, and tiny
>Romeo, still somewhere sings
>And, the found old connection
>to the nature
>that lives
>Lights the way

... but, the precious innocence gone?

Raining Soon

>I know
>you are coming
>Feel it
>from a distance
>
>It will rain, soon
>lightest drops
>or, a storm rising
>Just hoping, not a monsoon
>arriving
>God, pleased to see you, too
>
>It will always rain
>when you are coming

Apples in a Tree

Being picking
those apples
for years, after years

But never seen
nothing like
in a tree, of thine

Just a silent wish
and, a smile
soon, its all mine

Rose that Whines

A rose was whining
behind, and hidden
it was all shining

Should it be given?
already dared, and shared
perhaps kissed
A romance, on a whole new level

Maybe, not yet
it might get better
even hotter, and perhaps wetter
Like the longest love letter
saving the last line, forever
the next time, never coming
So, the Rose kept whining

Proposal

Would you, please, dear Darling
    all the shine
        and, eternal peace
    Accept, a humble proposal of mine?

Take my heart
    Your Beauty, and the Light
        and, turn it
            to a stone, and jewel
    So precious

A new masterpiece
    for thy collection
        a diamond, your Highness
    Its lux, and brilliance

Your Highness, and all the shine
    one more jewel
        perfect among pearls
            for the impressive crown, of thine
    All yours, to take

Shall I kneel, into thy feet?

Rocks of Diamond

Hey!
    why won't you check
        and, watch these out?

What is it, now?
    dear darling of mine

all the lovely shine
    Sparkling, and dazzling eyes

Here, they are
    these miraculous rocks
        pure magic, stored into the solids
    Secrets they hold
        old story, once told
            then, hidden and forgotten

Now, found, and I hold
    all the hidden charms
        spinning inside
    And, always rolling over

Like weighted dices
    the stones are
        making life, feel like a gamble
    And, what the player really wants?
        but to win, or
            the sense of excitement, of trying so

But hey, great gambler there
    be aware
        strong magic, awaken
    Let the stones roll
        thus, if they ever stop
            to think, or even hope
        Whole house starts turning
            walls, and all stairs, falling
                and, babe
        Who, wins then?

Better just roll em'
    their nature
        the reflection of light, they give
            should form a ring
    Tale tells

they belonged to an old king
   who, had same shaped crown
Roll em' right
   And, the rocks will speak
     pray, and sing
It is a word of god
     ... and, the secrets shall reveal!

Or, so the tale tells, dare to try?

Game of Poker

So, one by one
   she revealed it
     and there, it was
       a beautiful straight
A great hand
     with a King, and a Queen
       and, almost a flush
         but, by fortune, just almost
Don't rush

Anyway, what a great hand!
   she flashed her smile
     behind, the sight of two suns
And, a high pile of money
     all-in stakes, on a table
     started shaking
Leaning towards her

So I, yes I
   by the way, very nice
     finally, to meet you
       in these circumstances
         against all the odds?

So, I know, two cards of mine
both lying, down there
open, on a green
Cards smiling, on the table

First, the Ace of Hearts
facing up, the smart
the one, and might
lacking, the warmth of Queen
And, the second
the Ace of Spades
alone, so alone
as the Aces, forever are
and as great, as only Aces do
All the odds
of course, it is Spade
just the opposite
the red of Hearts
And, with only these cards
this hand, I will lose
the tower, of money
Seems to grow with its height

Still, three cards
turning backs
hiding behind
charming ornaments
And, I take my chance
slowly, raising one
and seeing ... a cross
Oh, my dear goddess!
the Ace of Clubs
all the fortune
whirling, the world
I must love you, fair lady luck

So, there you are
with the three of Aces

and still, losing it all
And the dealer, smiling
oh god, who is that?
dont' ever trust, stakes too high
Given, still two, precious cards

And, I inhale
don't dare, to see her face
rather stare, the green table
And think a lot, goes very close to religion
while I turn
my fourth
It is ... a Diamond

Diamond
I could do it, now
could have it, all
Take the pile of money
and just say, sorry
for the dear, honey
Would that be great, and fun?

It is the Diamond
and seems to be a ... Queen
the Queen of Diamonds!
On my hands, now
And, the world freezes
turns, upside down
Queen is a beauty
all the cold of the beauty
as, in this game
It is for nothing, the greatest nothing
most beautiful of a card
for nothing, nothing at all

By a twist of fate
faint smiles of Moiraï
it happened to be

A diamond
  also, in her hand
  just a Jack
The Jack of Diamonds
  squeezing, his sword
    holding, the mighty axe
Romeo, please
    shake thy spear, and ease
      there is a game, so tight
      close to fear
Must be, the cruelest tease

Thanks you, Jack
  and, the three sisters of fate
  you have given me
The slightest of hope

Anyway
  it does not matter
    matter at all, in heart's call
She had most Hearts
  on her near a flush
    in her straight hand
The might of King
    beauty of the Queen
    and, all the rest
Hearts, Hearts, just Hearts
    she was
      and, also
Almost, all of the cards

But, the fucking Jack
  the Jack
    was one of the Diamonds
How close
    was that, to
      a certain win?
The Straight Royal Flush

All the contradictions
and, overwhelming inconsistency
for her, opposite there
behind, the table green
Jack could have been
just, an old horse of queen

Lucky me
anyway, it didn't matter
matter at all, in this call
With the hand, of three
I was still losing
losing, it all
Lady luck, now, please call

There was still one card
bending, over the green
hiding the fortune
covering, her face
please goddess, let it be ace
But, all the odds
of the strange, five card world
would be against it
All the mathematicians
ever wondered, on our dear planet
would bet, against it
All the money
cash and gold
jewels and diamonds, they hold
Dear physicians
like the beloved Tellus
would suddenly stop
And, start spinning withershins

And, there I am
with my three
the Aces facing the cardinals

holding my faint hope
Now, to a Jack's helm
elbows down, on
the table, made of elm
Who rules the green realm?

Just a blink, the upstairs
don't want to see
the smile of greed
just right now
not now, please
What can man do?
What is he able?
all the money, on the table
and, the last red-back card
Odds against you
and honey, a hell of a pile
road of future, and fortune
covered with the tile, of money
Sliding out of the reach, of arms

I don't breathe
no more
no inhaling, nor exhaling
Just the last card
oh, my goddess
and, the lady luck
Where are you, now?

There it comes
the critical point
and, the climax of the game
the very moment of truth
I have only a left arm
raising the card
as, I hold my Aces
In the right one

Now, moving slowly
get the hold
and, feel the grip
Hey, young Einsteins!
on the moments like this
the time really bends
And, as I turn
my face to hers
I finally know
The last card, faces the sky

What might the card be?
how did the game turn?
I can't read her mind
Still, the smile
not like earlier, I assume
or, hope?
Can't see her eyes
what is she looking for?
does she know?

Close my eyes, and just hope
can't see, no more
anything, anymore
But there was something
in her smile
that gave me
hope, hope, hope ...

Alternative End

So, it is turning
   the last card
     can't see, the color
      why is that?
Now, it shows
   as the shiny mist of thrill
   slowly fades
Seems to be red
   and, a Diamond
     sign, that feels damn good!
There it turns
   next to my Queen
     of sparkling Diamonds
   Seeming to be ... Jack

Damn, of course Lady Luck
   I will lose
     cause of Jack
The fucking Jack

It is a Jack, again
   always fateful Jack
   coming now
   with the Diamonds, of course
How, in the hell, can it be?
   two of em'
     on the table green
Check the pack of cards
   probably, full of em'
     cheating alarms!

Someone is fooling
   that is for sure
   the second Jack
     of Diamonds, now turning

*But hold on
  it seems to be, also an Ace
    from the honorable house
      of the Diamonds
Oh my goddess, what is this?
  have I fallen
    into a world of madness?
Two Jacks, too much
  for one mind to carry
    and, was there ever
      any real hope?
What do I need, the most?
  the Ace of Diamonds
    forever, of course!*

*It took time
  to clear the things out
    but the card, that now lied
      in the center, of the greenest table
Was the Great Fool
  and magician
    the one called Joker
Now, throwing Diamonds, on
  should someone call
    make a date, with a shrink?
The feeling is truly surreal*

*Due to his extraordinary nature
  and twisted, theatral character
    he was also Jack
The Jack-of-all-trades
  now standing
    on the green table
      with two feet
As great
  and, alone
    as only Aces do
But for a reason, or another*

he kept smiling
just like, only the Jacks
Fools, and Jokers do

Still, there was something
that can not be explained
just like, the relationship
of you, and me
here in the game
The card was the Red Joker
a great clown, and fully wild
always a trump, for the own kind
Here, showing to her
what does it mean
to be the Jack, of all trades
Pointing, his precious stick
magical wand, of a wizard
and, the scepter of a King
Towards, the missing Heart
of loser's hand
and, only the clowns
Are, forever laughing
For the lost crowns

So, in the end
time was truly bending
and, the tower of money
Fell, and fell, and fell ...

Cash is King

Cash is king
    you kneel
        and, follow

Cash is great
    you adore
        and, obey

Cash is god
    you crawl
        and, pray

Tale IX – Playing Cards, Not Enough

The hell is on a doorway even you did not invite it. Evil is rising now on another way. Too much time spend and consumed. The princess is bored, and tired of playing just the cards. She wishes a true demonstration of love, and well, now also power. She calls for rivals, like there would be a war, for it is her time, rise to queen, now. Is there a reasonable explanation, does anyone know why? No, no one knows that is for sure. If interested in the philosophy, just ask about it from the female life crossing all the species lines.

Anyway, who cares why? It's not the question here. The question is, will you play more serious game. Now, the princess – at all her beauty and bright – has found a perfect rival. And since then, has been so exited, and busy, with arranging a precious fight. Welcome VIP, and the star, you are warmly invited – with open arms and all the loving charm! There will be a duel, at a dawn, like in the old days ... must make chicks hot, someway? So, a fearless knight — just and right, with purest of hearts, you are ...

Duel, at Dawn

Facing a man
a foot taller, than anyone
and, the same wider
how else, it would be fair?
At a red of the dawn
fate smiles
and so, does the swords
Blood rushes trough, feeling so alive

Helms on
on days like these

knights are born
Only one woman, witnessing the fight
the lady fair, judging
an old game, soon starting
A light nod
of a her pretty head
all, that is needed

Steels of two shields
bang together, sound so fine
the other, of a roaring lion
and the other, of a standing bear
Nature's great, and wild
finally meets, and damn
that man is huge
Hence, when the fight starts
for a win, grow yourself
a foot, enough?
Not totally a mental thing, but it sure helps

The first side-swing of a blade so sharp
leaving a open scar, to the black of bear
quality steel, just cosmetics of the war
Why wouldn't I strike above?
the wizard, I call mine
it is a loyal friend
put, all my trust on him
a small fake, down
and then, a swing
aiming the head, and helm
The shield is on
only thing splitting
the paint of lion's mouth
So, the fight goes on

And the lady fair, judge and the care
just keeps smiling
or, might be grinning?

The very closest thing, to the tightest smile

Anyway, here
you have to earn
the place among the living
by killing
There's no voting, nor debate
no sharing
nor, mom Teresa caring
Only one king, and a dead body left behind

Odd is the way
we keep living
and dying, but who cares?
It is a second, or third round
and, who's counting?
the point is, no winner, no blood yet
Just exhausted fighters
leaning together, shields between
and a deep, vaporizing breathe
smoke playing, on a morning light
ghosts, negotiating with the fate
Fresh is the nature, when life is on a line

And you still think
the fight could go, over the night
just use the shield
don't be a fool
stumble, and fall
He hugs you, preventing a strike
starting to like you, already?
or maybe, getting tired?
Now, could be the chance
should try, take the blade
to a final wave
let the Wizard, do its magic
Tell the world, who's top of swords

With those thoughts
* I feel the numb*
*   spreading into the arm*
*   holding my blade*
A deadly hug
*   a dagger standing, now in the back*
*   to the old wound, it found*
*   and burns, like*
*   the hell risen on earth*
Trough the weaker side
*   of armor light*
*   the weapon of sly*
*   slides between the ribs*
Deep, into the flesh of victory

It crystallizes to my mind
* two options, given*
*   merciful fate, always listening*
Leave there, and die now
*   or escape, while you still can*
*   and die later, alone*
Man without his sword
* no man at all*
*   fierce god of war*
*   now, looking you down*
Hammering your shield
*   bang, bang, bang ...*

A light of full moon, watching above
* nice, green yard*
*   and the round, fighting ground*
A man swaying across
* beyond bushes*
*   and disappearing, behind a tree*
Only a street dog, barking, far away

It is all done, and over now
* fair, or no, no one will ask*

if you are dead
    does it even matter?
Do you even remember
    what, you were fighting for?

And, only a faint smile
    fading behind
        the last thing, the man seeing
And, a huge shadow
    now guarding
        the slaying ground
Could been, the graveyard

It is a red dawn, rising
    and, the following
        longest day, shall just pass

Tale X – Getaway

As betrayed once, loosed his heart and confidence, always under doubt, and perhaps just because of that, he lost the fight, or maybe, the opponent was just better ... or was it the princess who eventually stabbed him into the unshielded back?

Anyway
    a second time, a strike
        between, the ribs
And there, a dagger stands
    reaches, towards thy heart
        truly strange couple
They are

So, you choose to escape from a certain death. Honor or no, you are still somewhat alive. Lucky man, since you are not a samurai. Bleeding, but alive. Where shall you go?

Snowfall

A white snowflake
    swaying, slowly down
        landing to a gray of stone
Small star fallen
    for a moment
        making everything close
      and, smaller
Somehow livelier

Till it melts
    changes its form
        the ice-white crown
          to a liquid diamond drop
            rising, next to another one
A perfect couple
    on a morning sunlight
      oh, great and might
God has some style

Cold tear of sky
    sharing its shine
      to a thicker one
Mark of fresh blood
    and another, white star
      drops between
The red, and aqua

Only few feet above
    the same thing, repeats
    on a trail
      running, towards sky
On the mountain highs
    where, only god
    asks why

White of ice
and, red of heart
tears, that seen it all
Enough, will wash it away

And, a mile above
a man lying down
eyes given to sky
Light, starry snow
playing around
finally, falling down
On his helm, and vest
boots, and the blood-red sash
arm crossed, elbow to shoulder
Lying over his silent heart

Icy stars burying the man
knight, of the mountain
white is the chest
And, his funeral as it is best

A low, gray cloud
lingers, into the grave-ground
eternal wall, of the high hall
hides his shape
Man lying, on the mountains

Good man, now, Rest in Peace

Bird of Omen

Fieldfare's whistle
on a stone, below
and, a merciful look
over, opening valleys

Taste of a drop
   water of ice, choice of bird
    red blood, only for beauty
Into her black-pearled eyes

Chacks of grace
   And, a shake of its tail
    spirit's gone
     flown to wind
And, another one arrived
   landed, onto a gray
    of gravestone, above
     a memorial, waiting
      for its writer
       letters of blood red, chosen
   Vulture's sight
    spread of feathers, the black night

Scavenger's lands
   high above the others
    only bones, left behind
And, the black bird
   glides down
    to a bare of skull
     still, looking down
      between, impressive horns
       of a poor-faith, mountain buck

It is a graveyard
   for some
    but, the vulture
Looking over, the kingdom

On the Edge

It is a riddle
on a boundary
and still, in the middle

A kind of a riddle
Joker climbed, on King's saddle
here, the crown will be thrown?

I am the one
on the edge
Forever, as evil
as, I am good

For years, and years
been searching
what is truly yours
Wandering
on all thy hidden fears
surfing, on the spilled tears

Here, on the edge
I am always
as alive
as, already dead

Maybe, and just maybe
a second, or two
I am
as much you
as, me

To cut the truth
here, on the verge
between, the light and shadows
Forever, feels like now

and an idea, diamond clear
still, only the skyline
will tell
How far is hell?

Fall

And, I fall
fall, to my roots
both, red and blue
Green of leaves, and
the shadow, I am
rise, of night
and, the last of rays
Looking, my way

<u>*Path of Shadows*</u>

Tale XI – Into the Dark Side

All the good in your heart ... not enough. What you can say? The words won't help, here.

> *As a second time*
> *dagger stands, just backwards*
> *in his chest*
> *and, the good heart bleeds out*
> *All things turn*
> *evil alive, hidden inside*
> *rises, and takes the power*
> *And its dark force, now getting stronger*

Like the oldest story the life goes for you now. Perhaps, that is why the story has prospered so long; the battle is always there. Can't escape. Now, you are just on the other side.

Fallen One

> *To shadows, I have fallen*
> *into the dark*
> *the Giant turned*
> *Faith, hope and love*
> *where have you gone?*

Now, arm broken
    all the aches, of Achilles
        in an evil world, I drag my feet

Shadows

A thing, once told
    a warning, fallen into oblivion
        as the reason, in us grows

Don't trust the shadows
    they come from the darks
        can't stand the lights

Still everyman bares one
    a beautiful lie
        evil to fall

    As the lights, go out

Devil's Whispers

Coward, what do you crave?
    forgot it, fool
        all the feelings of desire
Are you afraid, sire?

Covetous, bare thy covers
    reveal it, wolf-eye
        the hidden secrets
And then, share my treasures

Hypocrite, spell your name
  heads, or tails
    anything genuine, left around?
Tell me, proud
  make it, aloud
    kind is my please
And, great the reward

Thee, half-heart
  remember
    colour of thine blood
Dark, even the red
  under thine hood
    stand up, and fight
Show the true colors
  half-heart
    let the people, walk all over you?
How low can you go?

You, small, not even a man
  die, and be forgotten
    or take, what belongs to thee
So, what do you wait?
  you nothing
    you have been shown the way
Now, just do what I say

Tale XII – Evil Taking Over

The thing is both mental and real. Turning to the evil side
changes the way you view the world. Even your memories will
twist. First doubts will crawl in. It is a suspicious world. Enjoy,
the dark sides of déjà vu, evil speaking in the shadows. Enemies
— life turned to dark, you normally wouldn't even notice — will
sense the smell of weak blood. They will rise from their hides,
haunt and persecute. They are crawling everywhere, waiting for
the fallen ones, and they are thirst for your still fresh blood —
almost innocent, just turned. And, that is just the beginning...

On the other hand, on fool's stolen heart, there is a war on
the world whether you want it or not. And it is not fair, in
anyway. There is no code of honor, to follow. And no, evil will
not get its pay — or actually shall, and much more than that of
the honest poor. If you fail to believe into such noble things,
soon killed is your fool's will.

> *Welcome, déjà vu!*
> *a twisted one*
> *the good died, and love's gone*
> *All that means, and slowly leads*
> *only, one thing*
> *from the darks, a war shall rise*
> *soldier, just for you*
> *Mars been waiting*

So, you were dragged to a war. People haunting, and
persecuting. How do you survive? Will you grow a thicker
rhino-skin, poisonous words and sharper teeth? How do you
fight the evil, and win. Change your skin, like the snakes do. The
dark side draws you in the game; more evil you are, stronger you
feel and beat the others. So, you rule and survive - this is how
the evil spreads, and evolves. The dark side is now twisting your
mind. Here you go ... to the cruel world of war.

You already lost the shield of fair, for the mountains, and the sword of right and wrong during the duel. The sword was your backbone — honest and just — and now, just like a lizard on the ground you lie. Well, to look the bright side, in this world you are not alone ...

Evolution of Evil

It starts, just with a thought
    first act, and a change of attitude
      manners, and behavior follows
        now, character already twists
As evil slowly dives, deep into the values
    it reaches the genes
      your offspring, eagerly waiting
        evil ready, when they are born
These kids, don't even need
    customized way of ill-treatment
      as the evil spreads, inside out
        throughout, the society
In the dark, evil rules
    and the light, on the edge, it desires

Greatest Liar

The greatest liar of em' all
    leaned back
      and, once upon a time, forth
Just to go
    deep down, again
      eyes half-closing
A birth of a divided world

And there it was
   a long lizard of an ancient world
      a great beast of the underground
Most magnificent creature
      able to cut worlds, into halves
         now, crawling into sights

Casting a shadow
   long as that line
      of thy precious life
Does the beast mind?
      under the light of sun
         it seems, almost, kind

There it lies
   the greatest treason
      ever lingered
On the surface of earth

Once, a curse was told
   deception had crawled in
      snakes into the veins
         poison into the consciousness
Since then
      evil shined, through its eyes
         feeling too god, to be true
            beast in the highness of its own
Be aware, a very infective disease

So today
   it was all, again just a lie
      like that stone pile
Dancing around
      with waves
         dying on shores of bays
And lizard, well knew
      should soon, choose

once more
Between good, and so seducing evil

And so it happened
with a swing of the tail
betrayal bled in
Written deep into its nature
waves of white lies
descended on the shore

In time
the sharpest teeth
ever given, to a cheat
Grew, around a long, split tongue
the strong, white bars
cutting the truth

The greatest liar smiled
it was all a lie
here, even
The dead was alive

A war, had just started

War Lord

There is a war
on a shore
Rules are changing
people hunting, and killing
homes escaping
Who cares, what you know
or can, anymore?
choose your side
or, escape

A war is here
  tribes are fighting
    racism spreads
      humanity, on flames
It is the civilization that fails

Wartime
    on our doors
      stone broken, windows
  Blood, on our footsteps
    take care
      choose your side
        and then, just prepare to die
  On a war
      death is knocking
        on the front door

Soon
    whole shore
      on fire, under the fight
It is a party, call
    all criminals
      break the walls
  Rise of thieves
      blood on their teeth
        evil streams
  Red are the streets
      riots, on the squares
        smoke, and flames
  Dead, and injured

No rules, nor truth
    no honor, code of any kind
      bless the crime
  Anything seems allowed

Kill the opponent's best

and, slave the rest
Here we stand
on the very brink
of everything human
Hard edge, of steel

Mars, you
liars, and thieves
and, all slave lords
Escape, the free worlds

Time is for the war

Flee

Chose to flee
escape
and climb, the heights

Dark, now falling
all houses burning
a rush hour, on graveyards

A war, down there
ruins reign
a lust of power, triumphs

Persecution remains
a delusion ever stays
collective illness, easily growing

Up here, still feel free
even, the heat evades
and, the cut roots bleed

Have I lost my soul?
  pureness of my conscience
    down into the dark, I peer
Shivers, going through, me

Tale XIII – Thing, you can't escape

So, what happened? You were supposed to fight and go to the war, kill and steal, anything you can. The dark twisted you, gave you powers, and made you strong. And still, for the devil's headache, you chose to run, and escape.

Weak, they mock you now, and a traitor you are, of course. But there is no way; from this war you can't escape. The war has its soldiers everywhere, and you don't yet have any idea what kind of cruel enemies of evil, grown children of the war, you will still face.

Black Widow

In the darkest deeps
  devil following
    your path, and thy choice
Value for evil's deeds

And, now feeling
  that, it is the time
    and, has a perfect quest
To end, your miserable trek

So it happened
  that ...

With all her eight feet

down, on a web
  carefully, knitted by herself
Under
  all the cold
    and, dark of the nights
Distorted design, of starry nights

She had been betrayed
  so many times
    told, too many lies
Even, her offspring eaten
  under her eyes
    turning, her blood to poison
      and, her mind dark
Breaking the one, to pieces of evil

All deceitful schemes, rising
  perverted plots
    on eight feet, crawling
Mars
  up, into her fraud soul
    garden of hell, on flames
Growing, among us

Into the devil's mind, she could trust
  e'er right
    a silent war, always going on
      evil whispers
        and lies, her dearest weapons
Lethal shine, of the world behind her sight

Revenge, and respect
  she was screaming
    poison, out bleeding
What had been taken
  from her, stolen
    should no one else
      ever, be carrying

Death, she was dating

She was the black eye of the devil, now
the weak, and fool, she would eat
proud, and the honest, she would feast
Anyone, coming too close
would be at great danger
but, what she the most enjoyed
was those poor, looking for love
And that was just, what she now sensed

She knew, very well, what had to be done
a little charm, and pretend
to be interested
Just shake of the feet, and an inviting look
turn around
and, look vulnerable
Pheromone into the air
irresistible perfume
and acting, the innocent
Hide the power, till it was too late

So, the trap was ready
the web waiting
and, venom moistening her mouth
There the prey came
all too close
soon, she would take her first bite
A neck, of an innocent
and a taste, of fresh blood
thirst, on her lips

She would bury this, alive
into the white
grave of silk
Tie the hands
feet, and mouth, too
and, suck the poor's blood out

The half-dead, would be her price
  more, the victim suffered
    more, would be her pleasure
Old beast
    of the ancient world, smiling
      on both her firm fangs
Venom drops shining

Now, all eight feet
  open down
    marching towards
Four Queens, chosen
  in a line, dancing
    in her grounds, now
Only, a fool would come, if known

Showing up, first
  the queen of seduction
    like a princess, charming
      and fooling, the prey's heart
Taking him to a deadly walk

As second, hiding behind
  the queen, of revenge
    cruel one
      that would bite his neck
And, stab the back

Third, for the kill
  the queen, of pleasure
    on dark sides
A female form of a butcher

Fourth, the hungry one
  the queen, of blood
    forever, thirst
On prey, she feasts

And there, the fool
    of you, coming
        looking for a nice time
            and, a luck in the game of love
    Seeing only the first

Poor man
    only few steps, and ...
        devil, would have its price

Two Fangs

Two fangs, spoken
    fool's love, out bled
    Mistress, had a hidden lover
        for each, of her feet
            two, for each of her persona
    Deadly white venom, now paralyzing

To a world of paradox, you fall
    it is both true
        and so maddening, impossible
    How, can one be two?
        you fool
            now, the poison
    Rips your mind, into the two

The feeling is paranormal
    it does not help, much
        but, the philosophy
            is the very same
    The life, was once born

Cursed

Cursed I am
walking the line
just backwards, all the time

Cursed, and damned
carry my jail
against the day
all the way
To a dawn, I reach
never, getting a hold
black magic been told
And the feeling, not e'er old

And as cursed, an inevitable follows
doomed, I am
bowed, under a charm
A damn spell, walking on foot
just a feeling
the time bleeding
out of all, existing
once mine, everything

Finally, the magic gone
a dead body
the deserted one
A fool
left behind
and a stare, for nothing at all
Passed king's hall

The magic had an evil name
written to a strange sign
leading to shadows of a stairway
But who cares
or remembers, anyway

the end follows
Only dead, left, on the doorways

Abandoned Child

Hey you, dear
child of mine
Get lost
not, time of yours

Hey you, dear
child of mine
Rise, and walk
not, place of yours

Hey you, dear
child of mine
Why don't thee
seek, something new
not foreseen, ever felt before
It is not, your place
nor, the crystals
on a floor
Just a quest, on palace's halls

Hey you, dear
child of mine
Go, and search
something new, you can stand on
to trust, and believe in
Ask, and listen, where is thy heart?

It is not, your home
not here, not now
go, and evolve

Hey you, dear
child of mine
Why won't you leave?
or, I will throw you away
let the dogs, eat the corpse, anyway

It is not, your kingdom
not here, not now
And, the dark shall follow
just to remind, thee, a day

No Chance of Any Kind

No chance
never, a chance

A small, young boy
just, a too different kind
always, the most unlike
closest thing to impossible, itself

No matter
what he did, talent he had
how hard he worked
or, good he was
In these lands
marked, he was
from the very beginning

And here
where, we proudly stand
Their kind
would never have a chance
of any kind

Tale XIV – Enemy of Thousand Faces

So, you are still alive? You faced the eight-feet beast of the dark and deep into the society code's written racism. You abandoned your kid(s) – one or two, and dwell in the world of boredom, mental isolation and desolation. And all that is worth of fighting? You could still go to the real war? Or you can adapt, live slow and down, perhaps hide. Is any other choice available, anymore? Toughened is your skin, spines growing already? And now, you certainly think you are at the bottom. Then, think again.

All Ink Gone

So man
> *what do you think?*
Now, when
> *all the ink is gone?*

Red blood, that turned to dark
> *been drained*
>> *creeks running down, the night*
>> *all the mountain, high*

Feel your feet
> *at the ground*
>> *ready, to root?*

Death, just a meter away
> *or thy mind, still flies*
>> *flies away?*
Far, far a way

Same Road

A year
   since marching
      the same old trail
Please
      tell me mother
         is there another?

   Sun, so bright
         growing soon old
            just watching the moon, cold
               going around
      The fool, I am

A day
   since walking
      the same old path
Please
      tell me father
         another around?

   Earth, always so thirsty
         soon, willing to dry
            just feeling
               the moon, tiding by
      Just old, and fool, am I?

Thief time

A silent man
   in the shadows
      the one, with the coldest heart
The greatest thief, of all time

a grand old chief
  a liar, behind the stars

The thief, is speaking
  should never have watched
    ever even viewed, nor stared
  Tried to lock me down
    wait, and see
      I will take all, that's yours
  In a silence, a crime was swearing

The king of thieves, among us lives
  a ruler, of unequal aspects
    a false lawyer, in the lands of betrayal
  Here, only cowards survive
    felony descends
      and, crooked dna prospers

In the deepest downs
  and, shallowest shadows
    the thief lies, forever hides
      and, his devious friends, sneak
  Hear you all
    the oldest language, speaking
      universal dialect, of falsehood
  Like a disease, spreading

The greatest of the teachers
  a well-proven practice
    over empty speeches
      time, executing the stealing
  Doing the very best, only a master can
    exploiting trust, and man's best friend, fear
      here, the faith is a poor man's game
  In the end, everything will be stolen
    nothing is safe
      time has taken
  The chief, king of the greed

There, the old mighty waits
for an inevitable taking
all thy hard working
being, only his making
A twisted master of cheating

There, the tiny senile, now down bending
all the weakness, and wrinkles wearing
a closest thing, to a genuine, humble smile
a set of empty promises, misleading guides
A hypocrite in disguise
it is a hunter's silent approach
the prey non-aware
a patience, is a thief's weapon
Let the fool, do all the work
close, towards walk
the trap is ready, and the cage is open
Now, the victim falling
soon, the time for harvesting
later, leftovers, just rotten there

It is the thief's moment
the very pure of his soul
time having fun, playing with your life
A robber, feasting on a treasure
taking your shoes, pants and shirt
all fruits of the hard work
The thief is speaking
for the first time
the truth comes out
Even the tone, is that of a lie

I will take all that is yours
life, and dreams
flesh, and bones
Make em' all mine
even the years, of yours, keep counting

leave you with nothing
In the silence, thief is preaching
dreams of greed, in the dark, grinning
you all, see into the liar's soul
Once, open for all, the world

The thief, always whispering
time, again lying
voice, not out of this world
nor present, in anyway
Just an eternal, unequal echo
cold, as it is old
welcome, evil in the house
no reason, will help
Here, the judge, don't even know, word fair

Truly a noble, among thieves
and as always, a masterpiece
a timeless diamond
and, the scattered light of deception
A crown of eternal cheats
true art, of making someone's yours
bow you all, hands on thy belongings
Thief time, a king of the most extraordinary
kind

The old antique
dealer of dishonesty
avoiding always, aloud speaking
That would be a great fool
leave marks
expose the treason, give light to the truth
let others, do the dirty work
A thief's soul
leaves a fraud's tone
echo of evidence
A history of mental disorders

Instead, spreading his lies
    silent wings for the ill rumors
        orders, for heartless slaves
            all bowing, the old, cruel and cold
    Teams of stealers, bandits and burglars
        crawling, in his feet, at his hours
            in his minutes, falling seconds
    Lost is the will
        gone, the fair of heart
            all just, taken
Kneel, the greatest of the thieves

A kingdom of the stolen dreams
    an old, grand master himself
        in a remarkable silence
            above all, of us
    Impressing
        the way, only fooling can
            till even that, feeling is stolen
                it was not yours, anyway
    Only the wisest of bearded men
        sharing, the crime
            the liar, and thief is time
    A king, and chief, with an adder crown

It is a perfect brotherhood
    only the greed, goes over falsehood
        snakes sharing apples, in our paradise
    As prophets have foreseen
        together they will carry, a newborn sin
            in the devil's name, Satan will prevail
    Pray poor people
        the evil, is in the house
            exploiting you, confidence of the
innocent
        House of lies, in the universal lounge
            must make you proud
                a great foundation

To build the future on

Great men failing
means mankind falling
thieves taking over
even hope, will be stolen
Tic-tac tic-tac
the time bomb waiting
and, the greediest eyes, just watching
And, waiting

Now, after losing even the words
dear busy gentlemen
wait a minute, and have a second?
There is still, something
deep, in the pockets
here thieves,
The last two, of my precious coins

Prosper! And, all folks – just Rest in Peace
May the dear thief, forever be, with thee!

Tale XV – Everything Stolen

Thieves sense the weakness, and the odor of submission. And they took their chance, stole everything you still had. Hey fool, thank the fate, and turning into the dark wars. Now, you are truly poor. Your life's work, every loved one – someone really enjoying, in the evil of the world.

Earlier, on the two-peaked mountain, you were on the edge and you fell into the dark. Now, at the bottom, what have you become? A filthy and despised beggar, now you are – with nothing but bad manners, and devil's spirit. War has taken its price, evil its share. Far are the times of lover Romeo, tall man of the woods, and fair knight fighting for his love? And twisted are your soul and heart. And, evil years pass by.

Finally, the fate gets bored on your behaving; and the evil shows up, to take its final price. On these desperate times, you all unaware, meet an aged blind man sitting on a chair in a gray of park. And he is speaking to you, or perhaps just to the coldest air.

Omen, he says
    you will meet one
        from the beginning
It will either kill you
        if you love, one
            or, if any evil exists
                both betrayal, and just, it is
Or then save, but only, for a good reason

Who cares what the old senile is mumbling? It comes not to your mind that only few years and you would look, and sound, very much alike. Anyway, you – a poor man – have nothing here. Only lots of envy slowly refining to bitterness, an evil cocktail for heavy drinkers – devil's lands, these are. As your last card, you faintly remember the utter greatness of the mountains, and the secret might and powers of the woodlands e'er calling, in the greedy mind of thine. So, the compass turns, and now points up to the peaks of the mountains. And, there is no coming back?

Dark Woods

Trough the dark woods
    up to the high mountains
        your evil, desires
Tall men of the forest
        watching, now you down judging
            evil grins, on a thousand face

Dark side of the green, you meet

And, no mark of life
    on your way
        gone are birds, with their songs
            deer, and goats of the forest
Even on fields, below the trees
        cows giving you, a bad eye
            horses, turning their backs
                old dogs sharing, only
                    warning barks
Like you would care?
        small world snarls
            lesser life, grates
Anyway, for sake of everyone, just leave

The sun hides
    clouds are drawn, by the dark moods
        normal chill, of the woods
            freezes, now the bone, and the hoods
Close your eyes, or defy
        and, just mars on
            above, the mountains call
                the heights, wood can't long survive
Over the clouds, the powers of gods
        evil e'er craves
            might of the highs
And, its favorite, digging your grave

And, when you finally reach
    out the dark woods
        to an open, stone ground
A crow lands
        And turns, its all black eyes, on you

Grim Reaper's Trail

Death was watching
    with two eyes
        evaluating

Between hills
    on a trail
        passing, through bushy terrains
    Under exhausting, tireless sun

Scheming sight
    and, the shine of lust
        deep thirst of life
    All scales, on razor's edge

A black viper
    rolled down
        between, two stones
    Only one thing, on its mind

Your foot, slowly coming down

Strike

And a strike
    two teeth
        penetrating through

Streams of venom
    flooding
        under the skin

And a fierce force

twisting around
and squeezing
The blood, going blue

And, I know
it is my time
seconds, going by
while breaking free
But, it is too late
Poison is everywhere
wrist goes numb
and, so does everything else
can't get a hold
Only, a beat of my heart

Tale XVI – Reality Calling

Oh dear god! That was the end of the man turned to the darks. Now, your phone rings. Someone might wonder how, and why? Anyway, you have a small meeting where your presence is certainly required - someone still caring the poor, and the dead? The gods want you down - as soon as possible - from the high grounds of mountains, and so do some of the people, too. It was the darker, evil side of you that met his destiny there. Pure luck, for you, that you didn't really love anyone - if you believe in the omens. Anyways, let us see what the meeting is about.

Reality Calls

Dear God
you promised
make us great
Did you forget?
a birth of life
and, all the evolution
here, we stand
and, wait …

Tale XVII – Earth calling

While walking under the shades and shadows, timeless dark path, reality calls. Asking for you, the fallen hero turned to evil's side, reminding about the current times. Let us see how the world seems without the shades of the devil. Still, a choice you can make?

Anyway, the real life is not only dancing on a bed of roses now. There are tests, the life sets, new people, and totally changed points of views. Will you cope, survive and evolve? Get wiser, and learn? Or fall, even deeper, to the shadows, arms of the dark, where you already are?

'A small warning!', the big boss is speaking. Check the number of your shrinks, before proceeding. It will be important. Do it here, and now. The life and big boss are thinking, and the nature following, most probably good and evil meets. They all wonder what to do, with thee?

To begin with it, first, you are of course …

You're Fired

Hey man!
   one thing
     please, come here
And, sign this one

You are Fired!
   your work, here
     is all done
You can dismiss, now
     clean your table
      and, make it fast
I have lunch to catch

By the way
   you are also
     well, dispelled
Our society, now closed
     take care
      all the fair
Dear Outcast

And with all the respect, never mind
    there is a new
     great, social playground
It is just for you
    with a suitable name
    hear you all
The diplomat declaring
    persona non grata
     here, soon leaving
For some, honorable men
    it is just party time

The wolfs are howling
  it is time for sharing

blood, all over the floor
scavengers, screaming
Their offspring needs eating

So, how do you feel?
now, that it is done
can you count
how many times, one?
I bet
a fool's fortune
not your first
Greed is thirst

Don't worry
I'll continue, here
just, copy your style
All you did
was fine
just now, mine
Thank you
so much
for all that long time
And close the door, when you leave

I am sorry, so sorry
just a turn, in the game
only one cut finger
a broken out of ten
More for us to share

Yes, and honest farewell
hand, on my heart
and, take care
I'll continue, here

Nothing Changes

Here nothing
   really changes, ever

It's the same road
   a tree
     and, a stone

Even, new year, already gone?

And, nosy neighbors
   one thing, to rely on
     they are always here
   Snooping, gone to unbelievable scales
     someone other been bored, too
       and, had a social breakthrough
         mind blowing, world-changing
innovation
   Spying, everyone around

But, nothing really changes
   just, the faces
     go older, suspicious and colder
   And, the wind blows through
     twisting, grins
       vicious gazes
         amazing, what human can
   Exceptional
     facial accomplishments
       everything, nowadays happening
   Around, on the hoods

And, you still
   keep thinking
     you're better, and smarter
   Somehow special

one of a kind
    like, everyone else
In their own world

The thought, just a faker, bored joker
    but, no one really cares
    everyone just sneaks
Nothing really changes, here

Dear Shrinks

Frustration
    failure
        and, a disappointment
One, after another

And here, we go
    aggravation
        and, the amplification
Annoyance, my friend
    the anger
        and, time-consuming
Growth of something, even greater

Bitterness, welcome
    finally proposing, melancholy
        marrying, and moving together
The state of depression

Dear shrinks
    please, bring
        all the medication
Available!

Tale XVIII – Hold On

Hey, hold on.
*   where you going*
*   a head mixing?*
Edge of a mental health

Welcome
*   the artists' world*
*   or, only a small step*
Into the illusion of insanity

That is the winning option, instead of the evil world? Please, check the brighter side – anything there? Or maybe, different kinds of people you need to meet, to light the way? Here you go with some of your friends and fellows, citizens of the world. Choose your side, and act your mate, be anyone you like, it is just a matter of choice and a small decision? You may not like all you face. But, just understanding the point of view, and opinion, might make you smile to our world on other way. Remember, god has a mission for you, and everyone?

Hippy Sleeps

Man, who in the hell
*   is that damn hippy?*
Sometimes, sitting
*   on my table*
*   on my chair*
Wearing my cloths

And there he is, again
*   a fucking lazy hippy*
*   that son of a bitch!*
Only thing, he is ever doing
*   sleeping there, and smiling*

like some funny thing
would be on, going

Hey, how work-shy
can anyone be?
a record, again!
In you
the laziness gone
into the other heights
And seems, it never lands

It really pisses me
never seen that hip
in a real action
Other than that
here meaning
doing anything
else, but laughing
and the favorite, nose digging
That lazy hippie
laughing aloud ... for us

Hey you, hippie
get a Job!

Sooner, the better
start now, already late
how about, a hair cut
and that, hat off
Give me a minute
and, I turn you
to a busiest hipster
downtown, ever hosted!
Or, something else
useful, and hardworking
diligent, to admire
Just a minute!

A noon
  and, a great surprise
  the hippie sleeps
  ... of course

Now, take a look
  hippy's wrist
  my lost watch
  ... or not?

Anyway
  that is the laziest human-being
  god, ever created

No wonder
  hippie takes the timer off
  leaves his hands free
Just to kick off
  the hardest job, hippie ever done
  raising em', behind the head
Call the police, and arrest
  the laziest guy on our planet

Goddamn
  pretty sure, too
  the hip steals my best
  ... cigarettes!

And, why in the hell
  there's my eyewear
  and girls, around
A fair deal?

Seriously thinking here
  someone just shooting
  the hippie
If it is not you
  then, it will be me

Hey lazy hip
stop wasting my money
and playing with my ...
What a ... that phone
just like to mine?
and, it is ringing

Ain't true
my favorite seat, taken over
hippies are ruling

Soon, everyone smoking
and, nutcases partying
under one fool moon
All furniture broken
bonfires taken
pretty much
whole society fallen
We need army
soon, it will be a war

Hell with it
it was my seat
we are all declining
The age of sloth following
era of apathy, rising
and ... listen
Someone snoring
I know, don't have to look

'Hippy keeps sleeping'

Pilgrim

An old man
    in the deepest downs
        on a sofa of his own
Watching a young man
    on a prime time tv
        doing the very same

'Why don't you
  do something proper, and soon?
    be useful
      get a ... job
        or something!'

The man
    loudest of the thinkers, around
        demonstrates the slowest of all rises
            so to say, rose
                with hardest of the efforts

Surely, in those tough times
    the rising of the cups
        all that happened, there and around
        anymore

So, it was a cup that rose
    or a bottle, who knows?
      probably both
        anyway, up to his dearest lips
For the fortune of mankind
    now, the man was happy, for a while
        smiled, and carefully wiped
            beard of cream, on his mouth

After
    ... a while

Or well, refusing to think
   it, as long as two
Certainly, a king in a living room
   we shall all, assume so
    rose, again
Marking his, precious, milestone

This was the beginning
   a journey of an originality of its own
    an expedition into the other world
     a game-changing quest, after his second
    ... favorite seat
The white throne, of his kingdom

Good Answer

'Teacher, teacher
   I know, I know'
 Screams young of a student
   rising his arm right
    high, towards the sky

'So, what do you know
   now, anyways?'

'The correct answer
   in the right way
    learned the lesson
     from the old and wise'

'It never really matters
   what I say
    or do, by the way
Only
   a great personal contact

*really makes it here
in many ways'*

*The young one spells
all the eagerness, flying on the voice
and whole generation learns
again, in this class
Evolution leaps*

Circling the Square

*A tree
yes, around tree*

*What, a tree
not three, then
around three, like
The greatest sequence of all, Pi?*

*No, I am sure
all my dear fellow mathematicians
that here
The question is, more like
to be, or not to Pi?*

*In a very essence
all the roots
lead to ...
Let me explain it, to you*

*Well
in these terms
and, hours of yours
we have to go ...
To the foundation of solution*

To make it
   briefly here
      the dilemma speaks
         rather than squaring
            the circle
               ... more about circling
                  the square

Like my dear
   and friend, Peter
      standing up, there

Anyway
   It is Christmas soon
      and, the answer seem to point
         around the tree ...

All it takes
   lights, and presents
      fights, and stands
         ... for

Three Men

Three brothers, three lives
   no work
      nor wives

Three boys, three minds
   small rooms
      and, great hopes

Three men, three bodies
   many stories

single status

Three citizens, three roots
free spirits
unknown roads

Dignity, that grows?

Non-Available

There is a meeting
yes, now
no, you can not
'The king is walking
with the Titans'
... you know

No, I, just an assistant here
want to send a message?
and, use your own phone
What is it that you want
to say, him to do?

Yes, reads em' all
responds to letters
roses, and notes
sometimes, even
Unknown numbers, of phones

So, what shall I write
a poem, or an invite
you want him to react, or do
a wild guess, contact and execute?

Would you like

to spell it here
or perhaps later, by yourself?

Certainly, my dear
so glad to hear
in fact, I am so sure
will, 'personally', come to see
'you down there'

Loves you, 'all', so much
can't even believe
yes, 'as soon as
the Titans are gone'

Actually, pretty sure
they leave, soon enough
shall I send, thy message?
tell em' to harry-up, a bit

Champagne, sweetheart
while you wait?
By the way
just a short notice, here
for your confidence, only
'It took just a month
for them to turn, around'

Why don't you, come
back later?
And, if you truly wish
'the king to return'
as soon as possible
For the needs of yours

Perhaps, you
all the sweet, and dear
in our world
Could kindly ask

'some of our pretty angels
flying him back
back, to our kind'

Queen of Conspiracy

By the way
you should not
tell your mother
She is always haunting
sneaking, and spying
probably, all the time, just lying

Dear darling
did you mention
her maiden name?
Was it, do I remember right?
something like
the Queen of Conspiracy

But, how nice is that!
it makes me feel
a bit small?
Perhaps, I need to leave
and, escape
vanish forever

It is freedom, now calling

Attitude Check

Check, the attitude
  and, walk through
    below, and above

It is not you
  check, the sides
    and corners, please

Not you, just a wall
  and, bars
    on a dusty, old window

> Son
>> don't know a thing
>> if not first taken
> Can't even aim
>> towards the heights
>> if not stood low, first

> Still, there are times
> those things
>> somehow, someway
> Don't matter, anyway
>> remember your heart
>> keep the people alive
> And, remember to live

Tale XIX – Tipping point

So Hamlet, your values changed? Surely, all will hope. And, you are still alive. Good to hear, my friend. How do you feel? You remember Romeo, and how he was, or anyone else remarkable on your way, a loved one and the giant perhaps, shrink and the hippy that sleeps?

Now, into the grey, casual life, you have fallen. Your soul lost, or still grows? *Is this all, the miraculous life offers, till the final days, till the last moments?* In this strange world, what is your role, why you were made under the blue skies, now so grey? 'Are you going to survive?', the earth always asking. Let the gods do the thinking, suggest you to take a walk, or a travel ... a new adventure, and just time outside ...

To make it here, a different point of view, you may need?
Remember, travelling and nature both having ways of keeping
your soul clear – if you still have one?

A New Man

I really hate to say
but on days
like those
Leave
the dead behind
and fade away
Walk up
those hills
all the thousand miles

March, like trees do
leave your sins
Let em' dry
on the rocks
... you move
Rise above
heights of open souls
and, have a meeting
The Gods, for thee, been waiting

Then, come back
again
as a new man

Hunter's Trail

Man walking on woods
  the oldest path
    known to human

A hunter
  with a light of foot
A soldier
  with a step driven

Basic instincts, awakening
  somewhere, lions still roar
    olive branch, in a wind, bends

A spear
  down, on the side
    on a straight of an arm
      guiding the way
And the nature, follow

The day is long
  but so is the way
    better, just keep going

Tale XX – Fairy Tales

So hunter, you taken off, left the grid, broken the windows. Feel the fresh air, and more alive, now? Remember, it is also about the philosophy of life. Sometimes, walking on the woods turns to be a surprising fairy tale. To such a world, you are now drawn – think it trough, lessons to learn, or just delight to have?

Name a Price

Tell me
old, and wise
head in pledge
Is there anything
a bird
would trade its wings?

The talent, of flying
rising to skies
gliding in the air
Staying, and playing, with a wind

Name a price
any fortune, on grounds, enough?

Valley of Green

So, mister Woods
how are the moods
green, under thy hoods?
A favorite greeting of his

But now, a great valley
all green and fair
open, over his eyes
And he already knew
forest had it all
green treasures
decorating its castle halls

Fifty shades of piece
and same in anger
love and despair
All, you can believe
the same, that you feel
in green, and shadow

And a great was the view
liveliest the green
light and dark
All smile, and shadow
shivering of the leaves
and a wave, of infinite shades

Truly a breath taking view
feeling of a greater force
an old wisdom
And a natural freedom
above the great valley
the green kingdom

And a whisper came
through the green of the woods
a light blow of wind
Messenger in the air
shivering the leaves
and a humming voice

'Why would thee not
spread wings of thy

and with me, fly?'

And he felt
    a burden, on his back
        rising from the grounds
    Strength, of great wings
        a leaf feathered force
            ready to raise
                only a step, from the air

Of course, man could not fly
    featherless, were his arms
        wings, just an old thought
            an ancient memory, being

But two small birds
    heard and saw
        flew, out of hiding

'Why would thee not
    walk with us
        up the hills
    Through, the green of garden?
        we will be thy wings
            and guides
    Eyes, on the skies'

So the man, got on a hike
    up the hills
        the green of a mountain
    A highway of stones
        path of the rocks
            the gray and white, under a green hood

Now, the man, on his foot
    this was his home
        under his hat
            these, were his hoods

Steps so small, and smooth
*   featherless wings out, on the woods*
*   dragging a cloak, of the green*
Up the hills, few foreseen

Finally, a mission in his boots
*   he was walking*
*   and aiming high*
Over a bare of roots
*   a trail*
*   flowing up the hoods*
Only, his breathe thickening
*   as the path, kept steepening*
*   easy first, the mountain suggesting*

So, step by step
*   he walked, on the stones*
*   left and right, and all again*
*   thousand times, and beyond*
*   like a train, its speed taken*

The birds were guiding
*   singing, a beautiful song*
*   telling the tales, of the valley*
And, a magical mist of the green

Finally, on the beautiful way
*   with the whisper of trees*
*   and help of the birds*
He reached to a point
*   secret of the forest*
*   taught with the green joint*

It is a moment
*   the stones start speaking*
*   sharing emotions*
*   basic feelings*

Old memories, and wisdom awakens

It happened to be
that all were on the mood now
smiling for his journey
Under the green, and Her shadow

Man had finally arrived
a quest, in the lands of wood
praising the green, and good
The ancient gates were open
a magnificent ark
in the gardens of the green
A flooding of life, in a sacred park
now a giant, slowly walking
in the Valley of the Green

On an opposing wall
on a high hill of pines
a familiar face was watching
A wizard, forever guarding
a pair of vertical cliffs, the eyes seeing
and a cave, speaking its mouth

And, as they stared
each others
the men of the valley
The wise, on the wall
shouted out
and blew, into the air
Called for the wind, and spoke to the valley

After a moment, or the two
the air came
filled his lungs
Slowly and deeply
as deeply, as you can say
while watching, the blue of the sky

Soon, he blew it out
and, a wind came
over the valley
bended the trees
shook all the leaves
So was the valley breathing
its green speaking

After a while
man continued his journey
for a moment again
feeling his step light
his heart pure

Light of the wind
song of the birds
and all whispers, of the trees
kept him walking

But nothing, comes for free
in this broken world
the nights are cold
and the rocks hard
That he stones knew
and demanded their fee
the entrance ticket, to their world
'It is something you carry, we desire '

And suddenly
a sweat came
hot of his red blood, pushing through
Drops of salt, emerging
bleeding, and falling
down to a dry, forgotten soil

'A thing was taken
out of us stolen

needing, to be restored
Given back, and then forgotten

Follow the path
  our faith
    share, its fortune and fate
  Foreseen
    just believe
      then you will understand'

And the water, kept running
  all its rivers, flooding
    salt of the oldest seas
  Bleeding, and drowning
    down, to earth
      drying white, onto the stones

'That is the price, for reaching the heights'

The green of the valley, felt
  and saw, all
    sent her word
  So, white of the clouds came
    a wind carrying em'
      against the walls of the valley
  White walking
    to the green
      under its skin

And a misty forest, appeared
  a mystique of a grey
    lingering around
  Now, the sun was gone
    palace hall gone smaller
      its eternal walls, fallen closer
  The times of ancients
    honoring
      the quest, by a visit

A lost myth, of the sacred path
    the birds, had been singing
    the trees, whispering
Indeed, he felt, and kneeled

Time goes by
    but finally
        the reality strikes back
The hour was long
    the sun was gone
        and, so was the path

Into the survival, he hang
    there was a task
    a mission
Up to the mountains
    his fate was calling
        above, the green of valley
        that was his destiny

Anyway
    here, surrounded
        by the misty walls of grey
Every path, seemed the same

Fortunately enough
    the birds were still singing
        guiding, and signing
            an old language whistling
To the trees, they were speaking
    stone to stone
        branch to branch
        flying, and waiting

After a while, and upward mile
    deep was his breath
And almost sweet

streams of the sweat

He did not know
nor care
he had been running
Already, the time given
under the spell of green
the charming sight
stones had foreseen

And the man, ran
his heart out
just like the fair, in horses do

Thus, here
in the mist of the green
secret garden of mystical grey
The time was lying
just, around flying
all thoughts, even soul, stolen

That was the great magic
in the Valley of the Green

Now, and thereafter
man was lying, among those stones
dried out, staring the valley
A mist, slowly fading
and, the green again shining
open was his mouth, and dead the eye

In the end
the Green
his beautiful Queen

Heart of Earth

Sweet sweat, and all the tears
belonging to earth
coming down, from the heart
The great blue calls, home waits

Halls of Blue

An old man
somewhere there
perhaps, back in time
or, in the future, who knows?
Sitting on an edge, of a cliff
facing far, far away
to the finest of lines
between the sea and sky
Only a moment
and the great blue
about to make a move

Once more
raising his sight
laid his eyes
up to the skies
Till eyes wide shutting
let the day
do the thinking
And the dark arrived
came, and met him
the dark of the stars

'Forgive me, please
I do not know

what I am doing
Forgive me, please
my sin, my pride
only fool of my age'
Whispers for the night

With the blind of his eyes
he fell down
to a free fall
Escaped the gravity
down into darkness
a long dark fall, out of heaven
The blue stairs coming down
into the nothing
a leap of faith
old and wise, might say

For a while
there was not a thing
till the gates of the great blue
A door opening into the sea
the warmth sucking in
into the hall of the blue
The lights were on
in a hall of the blue
and he got his sight
both the eyes, back to life, again

The sky was different here
all swinging of a blue mist
and the waves, on a silver roof
Here, in the chambers of blue
Poseidon was the king
and gravity the fool
Then, a voice around
someone near, and far
perhaps, the great blue itself
Whispered to his ear

'Only the stones
shall sink
within these blue walls
in these heavenly halls'

And he felt no weight
no sin, of any kind
if there ever, were any
He did not remember
where he came
nor even care, no more
Just walked in, trough
the doors of heaven
dived, into the angels' world

And the lights were truly on
in the beautiful hall, of the blue.
even the angels, still missing
Or, who really knows
maybe, he met one
called buoyancy, the love of blue
'Oh boy ... '
what a feeling
almost, like a first love

All smooth, and slow
in the beginning of a journey
in a world, of fish and octopus
And perhaps, the most unexpected occurred
they all came to see
with their curious, bright eyes
'Who is that
entering to their lands
into the kingdom of great blue?'

Ocean was alive
the blue had been nothing

but waiting ...

And when he finally
    raised up, out of the sea
        from the healing salts
He was a man
    with age no more
        nor past of any kind
A new man, was born

The salt, still, tasting on the lips
    the man just had a glimpse
        one of the finest, a world under waves
The blue, telling the origins
    the lost grail, blue one
        and the fountain, of youth

All the wars, and meaningless crusades
    now the night, already dark
        stars walking, into the park
Silver floor, and mystical shadows talking
    trees climbing, up to the sky aiming
        a young of a man, a light of a foot
        and a bird flying by
With grace, he greeted
    a rise of a lovely moon
        now, guarding the world

Later, maybe very soon
    somewhere there
        or perhaps, in the future
A young of a boy, on an edge of a cliff
    facing far, far away
        shared shortly
            some fundamental philosophy
The beauty of the view
    watching back
        both smiling, and knowing

'Perhaps life, itself
    was once born
        near a distant beach
Next to a beauty, of a shore
        in the arms, of the great ocean
        in the hall, of the blue'

Toast to Life

This one goes for the life
    Salute!

A drink, from the waters
    a glass out of ocean
        flooding of the sea
            tide over the bay
                all rivers, and lakes
    Running trough

Be the air
    a breathe, of the wind
        the lightest blow
            breeze out of sea
And, if you wish
    a fortifying storm
        hurricane rising
            monsoon to come

All the sadness, and the joy
    you wish to cry
        man, come down, from the clouds
The sky will be clear, and sun smile

White Diadem

A wind, and a breath
the sky opening
far away
And, the light of sun
rays spreading down
diamonds, on the verge of clouds
Horns of a white crown

And, a feeling
the growth of hope
and, a forceful freedom

Now, I know
where, the Lady in Green
took her crown
Diadem, all around

Tale XXI – Deep into the Philosophy

So, fairy-trailer of the old tales, what a nice trip to a living and loving nature? Anyways, it was the life telling the story – no need for a smoke, or drink, here. God gave you enlightenment, in the end? A moment! That might be a great blessing or an awful curse. Or, who knows, maybe you had both? To you here it means, that deeper into the world of philosophy you fall. What does it mean? Better just to go quickly trough, or think it very carefully trough?

Awe

From awe
I found myself
or, what was remaining
A thing, far greater
out there
no joker, no faker
Amazement
and, a humble acceptance

Trust me
it is a step of faith
leading to hope
Moving mountains
and, even
wakes up the dead

A need, for renewal
organize, and prioritize
rebuild the foundations
Identity, to stand on

I am both big, and small

slow, and fast
good, and evil
What do I really need, and want?
how do I survive?
where, I want to stand on?
Those might be the questions

Riddle in the Dark

So, in the end
who am I?
that is the question, here
To solve it, a personality test is given

Once in a while
hating you all
hypocrites, you are so small
It is the very reason
this one goes
for the pray, of the dead
Once, and for all
I swear
put my name, on a guillotine
And, on red of its blade

Au revoir!
closing my eyes
it is the mind, that sees
hears, through the fading tones
Fortune speaks
prophets foreseen
dices are rolling
and, crystal ball appearing

In this state

under a mental take over
  between the worlds, alive and dead
I fade away
  lose it all
    down to earth, I expand

I hear you move
  on a distant shore
Beat, of thy heart
    on the dunes of time
  Deep breathe, of thine
      in the crests, breaking
      The sacred wings, spreading

Here, it all began
  dead came alive
    a stone moved
      for the first time

I still see you
  Father
And feel you
    Mother
  But this one goes
      for those, not alive

I leave you
  all green, that grows
    the blue, that sees

And fall
    back into the deep
      down and dark
  With that last wave crest
      breaking
        all seeing crystals

True Colors

Don't you see?
   the lions
      on my eyes
Don't you feel?
   the blue
      of my veins

Don't you think?
   all the colors, of truth
     will shine, the best
In the shadows, of the death

Ashes to ashes

Ashes, I've become
   back to dust
     and grains of sand fallen
A solid rock, I am
    hills, growing to mountains
      valleys rising, out of plains
Now, all the soil

Yet, just an empty shell
   of broken plates
    all blood drained
      warmth of heart, escaped

Here, in the shivers
   I wait
    for the first rain, and sunshine

Earth on Fire

Tale XXII – Will You Rise, Again?

'So, what have you now become?' Back to earth fallen, burned all around, only ashes left, into the air and wind spread? Waters flown out – earth is, always, so thirst.

> And, your soul
>   a wormhole taken
>   back to the garden
>   into the green paradise, fallen
> But, no apples for thee, now
>   just mould you are ...
>   life, and love, consumed
>   what is left?
> Who you are, anymore?

If you listen, hard enough, there is still someone asking: '*want to rise, again?*' After all this, that is still the question. Think twice, or more, don't hurry – it is, of course, choice of yours.

You might want to collect, and maybe select, the pieces together, first. One, then another, and there you would go ... Here, you hold a short spiritual guide, how you might make it again, walk through the world – follow the Earth, soon on fire.

'*Giants please, kneel ...*'

Some magic, and a sparkling idea, you may need? And, your spirit needs to be ready, that is for sure – so first, a word for thee, before from the very basics you start.

Life is a miracle
to wake, the body, up
you need to do, the impossible
with thy soul, and mind
So, dear magician
where's your wand?
the one of life, and miracles
Please, be so kind
break the boundary, which
should not be, even imaginable
Shake that spear, now

Word

A word
for the silence
written one, once
might, be the wisest
A sequence of signs
and, living letters
secret of ideas, they hold
All the essence

Here, a letter
you are
now, walk
Take a break
bend, and kneel
up, and rise
sprint, and run
If you wish, fly, above

Swing, and sway
  make it, to the end of row
  up, and down
    you might be crow
      eagle, and a sparrow
Dive, and rise, again
  the world of dragons
    screaming, thy soul, alive
See and listen, feel, don't hide

A mountain, rising
  and a breeze, over the seas
  forest, and all its leaves
A tree, that speaks
  stones, who know
    and, mould that grows
The one, great shadow, e'er follows

Wizard
  and a beauty, of brilliant witchcraft
    casting an awful spell, upon you
Breaking thee, to the smallest of pieces
    lightning, an idea
      both wild, and wise
        what, you once might, be
Strong charm, taking control
    squeezing, thy tiny mind
      and, what poor is left of the soul
        turn it, upside down
          and, making the left, right

  Feel, the line
    it will change, the way
      world sees, thee, growing
  And, in the End
      only, a point, on a sky
        bending, the heaven

Elemental

﹡ Thousand years
Alchemists, been awaiting
And, here, you are ﹡

Earth

I am the earth
    all, its blue
And, I walk in green
    with thoughts, so white

    I am the dark
      lights of fire
        and, sand of time
The weight, of a stone

Fire

I am the fire
    love, and war
      and, bleeding heat
A beat of heart
    and, all light, alive
      calling gods, out of hides
The flame of life

Water

From a fire, I come
     the blue
        and a mirror, I am

Deep, and the darkness
     all waves
        and, the sparkles
   Passing clouds, and basic moods

 Dreams
      and, flowing streams
         a mist, and a rain above
   Tears, and the merciful grace

Ice-heart
      and, the great sculptor
         mover, and a carrier
   The keeper of life

From the fire, I come
      a fire, I extinct
         a mouth, I am, and
            the wide eyes, of the world

All veins, of the Earth

Air

Invisible blue
  and, the silent dark
    a voice, and light sound
All over, the great hall

The one, you breathe
  full, and the emptiness
    that, follow
Wind, and a blow
  in the lead, and hollow
    air, I am
All around

Dear Earth
  to waters, I speak
    and fires, I burn
Lightness, of thy soul, I am
  a sense of a storm
    and, the evening calm
The shield of the world

<u>Saint One</u>

Tale XXIII – Open Soul

Hmmm... Even the Giants were asked to go down, for sake of the earth, and for your heart. Everything is crystal clear, now? Four elements, and a strange, wild idea shared. Perhaps, the old mighty assuming, more questions arising? So, keep your soul pure, and open ... *and, a sudden wind bends trees of the garden, and brushes the hair of the giants, telling and singing an old song, for thee*

Man of north
   and, son of south
      woman between
East, and west

Open your heart
   how do you know, who you are?
      where your soul is from?
Who gave you eyes, and why?

Listen, and let your heart feel
   Maybe, the old signs are just out there
      Take your time, and open your mind
For sure, building it, took more than a day

Saint Stone

A stone, on east
   hidden
      and, brought to west

A Saint One
   on a way
      always, returning day

A home
   moving, around
      Amor flying
   Arrow stored, into a red of chest

Fountain of World

A square
   and, a statue
      an ancient blade
         out of a stone

A peace
   and, liberty
      a crown falling
         through the air

A fountain
   and, a torch
      angels' chords
         waves beyond a sea

Blue Moment

The moment is blue
  king is leaving
    the sun fading
  His holiness, is praying

Down, a giant kneels
  it is the young, that sees
    search, the peace
  Freedom, out of the skies

Welcome stars
  and, the lover, moon
    here, you are
  The deepest state, of blue
    a great, dark blue ring
      and, a marvelous blink
        of a charming eye
  Holding a breath, of the whole world

Earth's blue crown
  as old as it is cold
    for a moment
      on the shoulders of our own

Heart of Stone

A man
  for his head, leaning
    just a thought, holding
      in a strength, of an arm
  A new idea, growing
    man, nowhere

sees everywhere
A meeting, in eternity

David's gone
kneeled, into white
only a shadow, behind
A great marble
out of our bones, carves
time around, leaves
The white freeze

The moment is fainting
it is God's painting
castles of clouds, building
White, over us, raining

A human being
and, a hold of a stone
in a loose of the arm
Rolling, it around
feeling, the weight
gravity, of its kind
And, how it is hard?
as, all stones are
now carved, and well cared
by the white waves
On shores, of the great blue mar

Slow, is the day
and, so blind, the eye
dear, sir, gentlest welcome
The philosopher's world

Rolling the stone
and, in time
opening, the eye
a mind, of the one
Once, I was alive, so alive

Red Star

Can you see?
   there is a red star
    on our backyard
And, a golden cross
    rise of the sun
     on a blue ceiling

Good morning, all
   hope is waking
    and the faith, following
Church is open, soon
    all icons, revealing
     god is speaking

Stones, and all the red soil
   awakening
    bloom, in a graveyard
A torch, given
    a flame, of eternal light
     to a lifeguard, in red
Rush, of earth's blood

It is a single beat of heart
   love rising, and over bleeding
    a temple under, the blue skin
There is a red star
   in the backyard

Crown

A ring of fire
    and, a golden star
Rising, out
        of all corners
            thy kingdom, stars
Gracing
        the brighter days
            under, the bluest skies

Yet, one question prevails
    where is the crown, now?
        on times, of the nights
Fallen to grounds?
        all its beauty, and tales
            jewels, and white, of the stones
Lost to the dark?

Left behind
    only a silvering
        green mark

Saint Air

I am nothing
    not a thing, at all
        and no thing, feels like me

Never been
    nor, ever seen
        nothing, I am
            a great, nothing

For you
   an invisible
     and, the silent one
For thy kind
   just a blind
     air, passing by
God, asking why?

A spell was cast
   no history, nor past
     you are the last
No sin, nor a wind
   no shadow
     left behind
No mark, of any kind

Walking the Waters

Empty and tired, I am
   a summer, under a sun
     all the thirst, and walls falling in

Here, in the air, I wish to die
   to waters, I dry
     salts, of the great blue
And, a saint, shot down
   unfair, of the world
     rained down
Out, of the shoulders

Dear god, help
   give thy hand
     even, a finger would do
     raise me up, please
Saint, willing to march

follow the sun
after, a golden bridge
blue of the ocean
half, the world
A blue gate, they say
and, a spiral stairway
heard it, before
To heaven, I believe

Waters, cool down
a fellowship, company with the air
climb, up to the clouds
white, and grey, of the world
A key, and a ring
to carry
a message to deliver
Secret sequence
and, a magic spell
a small piece, called
Earth's DNA

On a mission, now
a pilgrim, on its way
and, the faith is strong
strength, from the sun
There is a coast, on west, they say
a shore, with a beautiful, green vest
and a route, all sixty shades of the blue
Sanctuary
and, the holy eye
hold on
A hurricane, to come

A saint, walking to home
chains, broken
a torch, fiercely burning
Freedom, on its long way

A Living Stone

Tale XXIV – Phoenix

So, sacred is planet earth. But, the question is, how to get you up? The magic was done, the elements given, and the saint one met. You might be ready? *One of the giants – somehow, linked to you? – turns down to earth, and whispers, the way giants do, for thee*

Remember
Phoenix, you are
all signs, just rise
Ashes, and waters, on a stone
and sun's fire, around
all you need, is grace
And, a beat of heart

Life

Life
the one, moving
tearing you, apart
One, to twos

Let the greatest psychologist tell
there is a game
heart, versus kill

Please, hear
    Darwin, speaks
      and, feel
    The ancient philosophers, always thinking

Oh, my god
    it is the evolution
      that beats
   Breathes
    and holds, its jewels
      rolls, the stones
   E'er, like a day
    opens, and closes
      in the end, you will see
   The time will tell

Winter

And, a winter came
    the white was out
      pole's embrace
   Share of its grace

With all its might
    calm, and the cold
      cruel, and a storm
   Pure, and crystal white

A knight, in white
    and, a strike of sword
      whiteout, the storm called
   Shine, that blinds
    wisdom
      beyond, the minds
   Armor of snow, and ice

> makes the fight, vain
>   cope, or escape

The White Giant
>   here, to stay
>   on the north side, now
> Turning, the blue
>   aqua of life, into the white
>   for his wise, and the holiness
> Walk on waters, of crystal ice

𝒮pring

Badam, badam ...
>   feet down
>   in the shadow
> Gone to south
>   fallen, to grounds
>   hidden, the cold
> And, long dark nights

Now, the winter is leaving
>   still waiting
>   heart beating

>   Grey, and brown
>   dry, and yellow
>   calm, and the peace
> All the patience, I am

A rest, and a breath
>   growth, of the strength
>   buds, and sprouts
>   grow, and swell
>   stars, of the green

The sun, will tell

The first birds, singing
        opening waters
            and, a light warm rain
Waiting, and growing
            before a first step, taken
                green lightness
                    walking up, to north
As neon, I will rise
            few hours
                and, few days
                    up, I'll spring
            Hail the sky, the green is alive!

Green Hood

A strange thing
    not thought
        rather, felt

A leaf, swinging in the air
    a canoe, running in a river
        kind of a feather
            falling, out of heaven

A green mark, on a grass
    where, a lady once stood
        a poem, on her heart
A faint token
        the moment spoken
            nature's way, of caring

A language, of the trees
    whispers on their leaves

a farewell, for the pass
Feelings shared
    in a strange kingdom
        under a green hood

Knight in Green

A knight in a green
    gave an eye
        to a young of boy
A smile of sun
    raising
        his, colorful wings
So, where is thine
    blade of shine?
        how do you, cut the time?
So, short, and sparse

Have you not heard?
    song, of a curvy beach
    seen, the diamonds
        on the waves
White of thy almonds
    decending
        far, out of the ocean
Please, feel
    the shoreline, on thy knees

Soldier of Dark

A Soldier of dark
    turned, to a knight

wearing, the green
  Beyond depths
    behind the diverse, blue earth
      with all stars, universe of the night
  So, where is thine
    babe, and the shine?
      how do you, spend the time?
  The priceless precious, given

Have you not seen?
  a teasing shade
    felt, the marvelous shapes
      as, my mistress fades
  Charming shadows
    and, the changing colours
      as, my love, and life
  Sun, the bright, finally sets down

Holder of Light

A holder of light
  followed
    the mistress, of dark
  Only, a moment
    of blue, apart
      a dawn, on her heels
  So, where is thine
    dear, and lovely shine?
      how do you, understand the time?

Have you not seen?
  the silver, marking all
    under a giant moon, so full
  And, the peace
    under, my arms

or, the dreams, world of desires
hope, and freedom
Or, the hollow, waning crescent
turning, to a new moon
new day, and season

But, I need to confess
loving you, too
thee, give me a meaning
Closest of my lovers, dear darling

Air

It's me, in the air
can you hear?
say hello, and wave
It's me, in the wind
can you feel?
freedom, and the shivers
Please, don't hide
let me, brush your hair
flesh, and the bones
Make you feel, so vital

Take a breath
and, let me, in
keep you, alive
Share, the power of mine
please, breathe
feel, so light
Think, I should go
it is the laws
my values, I obey
A balancing force, I am

sure, saints
        will understand
    Divine, equilibrium

You remember
    the world, is huge
        and, I need to leave
    Don't worry
        a friend, will follow
            always, does
    Believe, it is not a sin
        I am here, for thee
            and, take care
    Now, I leave
            please, say hello, and wave
                I will shake, the leaves
            It is my peace

Grey Moment

The moment is grey
    mistress, fallen
        down, for thee, wonder

Grey, and the mist, I am
    arrived, far away
        beyond the years, you know
            to see, the kind of thine
    Wonder, and foresee
        what to do, with thee
            helping you
    Make up, thy mind

Welcome, the chamber of grey
    a peace

and a harbour, of safe
Time to think, and rest
thus, nothing, yet for sure
besides, the long moment
mirrors past, to the future
I'll take a deep breath
and, watch thee
all around, the grey hall

Living Heart Out

Tale XXV – Choose, the Bright Side

So, remember, just a sparkling idea, a tiny hint of a groundbreaking philosophy, you were? Hmm... lots of 'talking', since. And, with that pleasant thought, you hear someone singing silently into the air, and the wind finely playing the music

Take my hand, my soul
nowhere to go
nowhere, to hide
Everything said, and done
nothing to loose, just to win
rise up, from the grounds
And, live

There are ones, still hidden, that want to be sure you are choosing the right, bright side. Thus, while you swell, and dwell, of all the wisdom given beneath, *the Giant Moon turns to speak, for thee. Wants to share a story, or two, good to be familiar for the future.* Talking something about a philosophy of Tellus, mental and attitude towards the living, and knowledge of great importance concerning survival on the sacred planet earth. Even, you start to feel a bit sleepy, while the 'big thing' whispering all the great concerns out of his heart. But hey, now, let the Giant tell, what he has seen, wants you to hear, and perhaps later do ... *under a pale, silver light over the green hoods.*

Heart and Earth

Oh' my dear God
  I guess
    you already saw
Long, long time ago
  the bravest
    and fairest, of all men
All the strength
  and, bright, of the women

Measured them, all
  by their Heart
    thus, giving us, worth
The Earth

Meditation

Finally, here
  leaning back
    and, letting it go

Sinking, and falling
  the black hole
    of strange mind

Till laying
  on the great white
    sand of time

Among the stars
   now, my home falls

Good Lie

Oh, my dear goddess
   let me tell, you
      a good lie

You know
   those, bright stars
      above, the sky?

On nights
   they are
      ... all mine!

Just like you are, my spine

Swiss Clock

Staring the starry sky
   a black, open mouth
      and, a spider web, of all time

In the middle, of the night
   a mighty star, stood
      home of the superman
         under, the black hood

A Swiss Watch, clicked

first a round
    left, and then right

But, a second
    there
        might be two, here

Tic-tac tic-tac
    the time flies
        always, under the starry skies

A Dawn

Into the shivers, I wake
    a dog's sleep
        the cold, of the night

And, a dawn
    the purple glow
        in the east horizon

Before, the first beam
    a glance of hope
        till, blood starts to circulate

Moon Stone

The Giant's gone
    only, a moonstone
      left behind
And, a faint memory
    strange story, told
      odd magic, old
The moonstones, for worthy, hold

Look, at my eyes
    and, to the stone
      then, deep into a tree, above
Do you see?
    The Giant Tree
      speaking, thee
And, his fellows, on rock-cliffs

Look, to the eyes, of a bird
    and, to the moonstone
      then, trough the forest, next
What do you see?
    all thousand birds
      watching, thee
And something else, line more older

It is a precious gift, for thee
    the one, wishing you to accept
      in case, you ever might need help
Watch, and stare
    the hollow face, of a full moon
      on times of night
Then, the charm stone
    you carry
      close, thy eyes
And just dream, deep, of me

Tale XXVI – Giant Moon's Gone

So, the Giant Moon
   all gone
     with the tide, 'run'
Nothing to do
   nowhere, to go
     and, nowhere to hide
Only a feeling
   overwhelming emptiness
     even, the silver's gone
The hollow, of the moon

Just twilight of memories out of the ongoing oblivion, the old great stories *Giant told,* under the pale night – with a voice, wise and warm, and whisper, strong and loud. About a man, and a woman? Any lesson? *Who knows, just a ghost I am.*

Isle of Man

An island, you are
   rocking cliffs, and
     white foam, of the crests
Washed, away
   whole society, left behind
     isle, of isolation
From the grey, and blue, you rise
   reach the sky, green
     the pure soul
That is, who you are

A harbour, and
   a white boat, swinging
     in an easy-going desire

A reconnection, to the civilization
till, you remember
what you were, escaping
forced to hide
You don't belong, here
to the blue heaven

Cafe by the Sea

A cafe
down by the sea
blue is the key

A sign
chalk, and the stone
green that grows

'Please
on this gate
leave your sorrows
And all faked roles
lying
on the last treadstone

Calm down
the storm's gone
here, you are free
If, you don't believe
ask it
from the sea'

Line in Blue

There is a line
  in a blue
    so sacred, and fine
Far, far away
    beyond, the horizon
Ever watching eye
      between, the sea and sky

See the wave?
  blue, in its vein
    Ave, Ave!

A Cave

Weather is changing
  the storm rising
    show me, the map
Dear, and darling, all the green

A plan B, we need
  what, ever, would god do?
    create, ... and survive

A cave
  just few miles, away
    a hole, under a cliff
      a temple of the nature

Safe, and sound
  and, did someone say
    a marvelous view?
Sea, and waves, relaxing

Thor

On the storm, now
   in a dark of a day
     and, a lightning
      striking, through the heart

Ancient gods
   arrived, flown over the sea
     landing down, to us, hear and see
     remind, who we are

A thunder, exploding
   waves, and the voice spreads
     shakes down, the spine
      a direct connection, to a neural system
The oldest language, you will ever hear

Humble, you are
   respect is the feel
     on the foundation, you stand
      and here, the strength grows
The hidden, inside, awakens

Thor, on the move
   fallen to grounds
     standing, among us
      jaw above, and wings wide
       against the air, with the clouds

Hammer is thrown
   out of stone, the statue carves

On a Great Wall

Turning it all, again
    ninety degrees
        no more
    Reaching, for the closest liane
        and, hanging
            on a line of life, and
        One of the greatest walls

Wonder, all stairs
    lead
        to top, of the world

Deed depths of air
    and, all the sights
        among eagles
            the great wisdom, flies

Breath taken
    eyes stolen
        and the mind, paralyzing

Till the fine liane, holding
    breaks, and lets go
        a free fall, starts

Word out of Truth

The truth
    won't come for free
      it requires a heart
  May cost you
      a friend, and perhaps, a family
        the nice home
          take, even a life, of thine
  Kill, your globe

But the truth, just might
    bend the bars
      holding thy heart
  Set you free
      from the jail
        we keep building, around

Speaking, open heart
    might make you, re-feel
      a thing, from your youth
  How being truly fair
      makes you breathe
        fresh air, again
      Take, a year, or two, from you
          or, lie
            and, grow old
      Your heart is poor

What, do you think?
    God, might note
      or, would your soul vote?

Ghost

Once, in a while
I feel, being
just, a ghost

From, the very moment
everything, is
always, possible

Final Lines, Last of Words

⸲ God, please
save, the green
queens … and, the stars ⸲

Tale XXVII – A Beat of thy Heart

So you, the fisherman – and now, a philosopher and a man
of faith, and a friend of Darwin, of course – did you find what
you where looking for? You, lover Romeo and king, hunter and
a pilgrim, soldier in the dark, and a citizen of earth, did you rise
again? Did you survive, till the final lines?

If so, one old, and mighty, might want to know a small thing,
from the mind of thine: *'How is the beat of thy heart?'*

Back Now

You are back, now
safe, and so ... sound
on the sofa, of course
God, how else, it would be fair?

How do you feel?
even seasons, changed
and, finally
Everything turned, out, just fine?

The Man Lost?

So, in the End
one question still prevails
what, ever, happened to that man
left alone, heart bleeding
in the very beginning?

He died alone
found a friend, or a loved one
someone, who saved him?

Or, he evolved
and, his heart grew
Found, an old connection
nature, life, and earth
in the shadows
Speaking, to him?

Close your eyes
for a while
and, the secret reveals
The answer is near
actually, just here
feel, its beat?

But for a reason, or another
just that page is missing
all the evidence, lost
probably, devil taken
and, evil hidden
Burning, in the flames of hell

So, how the tale goes
is up to you, to decide ...

Tale XXVIII – Fate of the Fisherman

Somewhere on our dear earth, under a huge tree, below a fisherman's hat, a man is sitting. He is watching over a nice garden, and leaning back on an old tilted wood.

All the green
　　apples, growing in the tree
　　　ready to bite one
　　　　and, on that moment
　A wormhole appears
　　... your eyes, spears

And, the time bends
　　sun rolling, spinning you over
　　and, the moon tides
　　　great blue, rides
　All the stars of night
　　falling, on your arms
　　　the tallest, knight
　Can't escape, this fight

Hey you, Luke
　　you know it, already too well
　　raise, your hood on
　A new travel starts

"You know,
It is not the Words
You keep remembering
It is the World
They walk in "

Angel's World

Out of heaven
    a letter falls
      and, the words kneel

In a river
    a rhyme lives
      and, the sentences flow

In a fountain
    a poem flies
      and, the tales dance

It is an angel's world
    waters on fire
      diamonds thrown, into the air